Intermediate through Early Advanced Repertoire

SUCCEEDING
WITH THE MASTERS®

ROMANTIC ERA, Volume Two

Compiled and edited by Helen Marlais

About the Series

Succeeding with the Masters® is a series dedicated to the authentic keyboard works of the Baroque, Classical, Romantic, and Twentieth-Century masters.

This series provides a complete and easily accessible method for learning and performing the works of the masters. Each book presents the works in historical perspective for the student, and provides the means and the motivation to play these pieces in the correct stylistic, musical, and technical manner. The easily understandable format of practice strategies and musical concepts makes this series enjoyable for both students and teachers.

To ensure authenticity, all of these pieces have been extensively researched. Teachers will find a wealth of excellent repertoire that can be used for recitals, festivals, competitions, and state achievement testing. Many of these original compositions may be new to you while others will be familiar. This series brings together an essential and comprehensive library of the pedagogical repertoire of the great composers.

Succeeding with the Masters® begins with late-elementary repertoire, continues through intermediate-level works and also includes a few early-advanced works. Upon completion of this series, students will be well prepared for the entry-level sonatas by the master composers.

D1601755

THE
F·J·H
MUSIC
COMPANY
I N C.
Frank J. Hackinson

Production: Frank J. Hackinson
Production Coordinator: Philip Groeber
Cover: Terpstra Design, San Francisco—in collaboration with Helen Marlais
Text Design and Layout: Susan Pinkerton
Engraving: Tempo Music Press, Inc.
Printer: Tempo Music Press, Inc.

ISBN 1-56939-600-0

PREFACE

A Note for Teachers and Students

Succeeding with the Masters®, *Romantic Era, Volume Two*, is a collection of graded repertoire featuring the great masters of the Romantic era. These works build a foundation for playing more advanced romantic music. Pieces are introduced by short "discoveries" of characteristics of the Romantic era, while "practice strategies" guide the student in preparing and performing each piece. This comprehensive approach to learning style, technique, and historical context provides a valuable foundation for successful performance of all romantic repertoire pieces.

Two icons are used throughout the volume:

**Characteristics
of the
Romantic Era**

indicates the Musical Characteristics of the Romantic era.

**Practice
Strategy**

outlines a Practice Strategy or illustrates a musical concept that guides the student in how to learn more efficiently and play more musically.

The pieces in this collection are based on Urtext editions, which are editions that reflect the composer's original intent. From these Urtext scores, the editor has created performance scores for the student. Markings that were not clearly intended by the composer are referenced at the bottom of the pieces.

- Fingerings have been added by the editor.
- Some articulations and interpretive dynamic markings have been added to guide students as they explore the romantic style.
- Some editorial metronome markings are added as a guide.
- The CD includes complete performances and a practice strategy workshop. For a complete listing of track numbers, see page six.

MUSIC DURING THE ROMANTIC ERA (1800–1900)

Romantic composers, writers, and visual artists were interested in individualism, imagination, and the expression of personal emotion. Romanticism was a rebellion against the order and refinement of the Classical era. Many composers wrote programmatic music, which is music that is associated with a story, poem, or scene. Romantic composers often projected their own personalities into their works, in an effort to freely express themselves. The composer who bridged the transition from the Classical to the Romantic era was Ludwig van Beethoven. Romanticists spent time in nature, and made it an essential part of the imaginative thought process. The romantic composers were also interested in fantasy and the world of dreams. Famous writers were Edgar Allan Poe, Victor Hugo, and Mary Shelley, who wrote *Frankenstein*. Musical activity was centered in Vienna and in Germany, but toward the end of the century Paris became the focal point with the composers Chopin and Liszt. Some composers wrote *nationalistic* music; they were influenced by the folk songs, dances, and legends of their homelands. Therefore, we can hear the national flavor of various countries, such as Poland, Russia, the Czech Republic, and Germany. Other composers wrote about countries they had never visited but only imagined, and this was called *exoticism*. Musical *exoticism* depicted places that were remote, mysterious, or picturesque. Many compositions during this era were sensitive, poetic, melancholy, and sentimental; others were dramatic, heroic, and intense. During this era, composers wrote performance directions such as tempo, dynamics, pedaling, and phrasing marks into the score; and ornaments were commonly incorporated into the musical line, instead of written as symbols.

Franz Schubert, an early romantic composer, emphasized lyricism and romantic harmonies, while still using classical forms and titles. Robert Schumann used descriptive titles for his pieces and is known as a "poet" of the piano. The Russian composer Peter (Pyotr) Tchaikovsky composed much nationalistic music expressing the Russian spirit. And Frédéric Chopin raised the *polonaise*, a Polish dance, to an art form, perhaps in nostalgia for his native Poland.

Both harmony and rhythm advanced during this era, and the piano became the primary instrument for professionals and amateurs alike. Orchestras, commercial concerts, and opera companies were in abundance, and the vast majority of the population spent their leisure time listening to music. This was the age of the virtuoso, with audiences wanting to hear the amazing talents of solo violinists (Italian Niccolò Paganini being the most famous) and solo pianists.

Hildgardsberg castle in Germany, 1841

REMARKS ON PEDALING

In this performance edition, the editor has placed pedal markings as a guide for the student. Careful listening to the CD recording and meticulous practice will guide the student in how to incorporate the pedaling that suits the pianist's style, touch, tone, and dynamic range, and takes into consideration the particular piano that is being played. In three of the Chopin pieces in this edition, both Chopin's pedal markings, as well as the editor's, are shown. Chopin did not often write his desires for the pedaling in the score, but when they are present, it is wise to experiment with them, because they offer a great variety of ideas with respect to phrasing and color. Many of Chopin's pedal markings work quite well if the performer listens carefully. However, some markings will not work on the modern-day piano because today's instrument is much more resonant. Adjustments of the pedal will have to be made to suit the acoustics of the room, the touch and balance of the piano, the sound among the different registers of the piano, and the pianist's own touch.

What the student will learn in Volume Two:

Characteristics of the era:

Helen Marlais' Practice Strategies™:

Volume Two – Intermediate through Early Advanced Repertoire

The pieces within each composer category are arranged in order of difficulty, with the least difficult pieces immediately following the short biography of the composer.

TABLE OF CONTENTS

	Page Number	(CD Track)	
		Complete Performances	Practice Strategies

FRANZ SCHUBERT

(1797–1828)

Franz Peter Schubert was born just outside of Vienna. His parents had fourteen children, but only five survived—four boys and one girl. Schubert's father, a schoolteacher, started his own school. The first year forty students enrolled, but in the very next year the enrollment increased to 300! The young Franz, by the age of thirteen, had already composed songs, string quartets, and piano pieces. One of his piano duets, the famous *Fantasie in G*, was a twenty-minute piece with over 1,000 measures!

Upon completion of his schooling at the Imperial and Royal City College, Franz moved back home and joined his father as a schoolteacher. He continued to write in all his free time. His seventeenth year marked a milestone in his creativity: his musical output was one of the greatest in all music history, with Franz completing sixty-five bars of new music every day! He was, in actuality, a full-time composer as well as a full-time teacher. When he was twenty-one, Schubert was invited by Count Karl Esterházy to visit his palace in Hungary, so he was able to see where Haydn had worked most of his life. (See the *Classical Era*, *Volumes One* and *Two* for more information.)

Schubert was known for his lyrical melodies, and over his lifetime he was highly regarded as a composer of songs (for voice and piano). Franz wrote over 600 *Lieder* (the German word for songs) and used texts from the greatest German poets—Goethe, Schiller, and Heine. Within these songs, a great deal of emotion and drama is conveyed. These pieces influenced contemporary composers and musicians, as well as generations to come. Franz was known to be extremely modest and shy, and had it not been for his good friends, he might have been penniless. These true confidants held weekly concerts of Schubert's music in their homes, playing and singing his newest creations. These evenings were called "Schubertiads," and it was there that members of the educated middle class enjoyed the music of the day. By the time Schubert was twenty-one, he was able to give up his teaching at his father's school and become a full-time composer.

Schubert truly was a musical genius. By the age of thirty-one, the year of his untimely death, he had written well over 1,000 compositions. Schubert wrote theatrical and sacred works, pieces for mixed voices, orchestra pieces, chamber works, masses, and monumental piano sonatas and other works for piano. Two of his great symphonies are called the *Unfinished Symphony* (1822), and the *C major Symphony* (1825–1828). He left behind few possessions other than his music, much of which was not published until the nineteenth century. In addition to his gift of lyricism, Schubert was known for his fondness for changing tonalities.

In the mid-twentieth century, Otto Deutsch researched and organized all of Schubert's compositions. The letter D represents his last name. The D numbers list all of the works in chronological order.

Today you can still visit the house where Schubert was born! It is shown in the picture on the next page.

The house where Franz Schubert was born

A "Schubertiad" evening
From a painting by Moritz von Schwind

THREE WALTZES

The three waltzes in this collection are from a set of thirty-six Schubert called Original Dances or "First Waltzes," and were written during a period of five years, from 1816 to 1821. The first one, called *Melancholy Waltz,* as well as the second, are dated from 1816, the same year that Schubert and his friends decided to initiate frequent "Schubertiads." These were domestic evenings that combined listening to Schubert's music with socializing. The last waltz of this set was composed November 12, 1819. In this same year, when Schubert would write from six in the morning until one o'clock in the afternoon every day, his famous chamber work, the *Trout* Quintet, was premiered. Schubert's music is known for great lyric beauty and natural harmonic spontaneity, as you will hear in these three waltzes.

Characteristics of the Romantic Era

Use of traditional forms:

Schubert used romantic harmonies, but also enjoyed using traditional forms and titles. The title *Melancholy Waltz* was given not by Schubert but by the publisher. Notice the binary form in each piece. All three waltzes may be played without separation if desired, as if one were playing for dancers during an evening of social entertainment.

Practice Strategy

Voicing the melody:

In all of these waltzes, it is important to bring out the top melodic line in the right hand. To "voice" a melody means to bring out one of the voices in an interval or chord that is played *within the same hand.* To hear the correct voicing, play each beat very slowly, making the top voice's tone full, rich, and *mezzo forte.* For the lower voice, make each tone *staccato* and very soft, as shown below. Feel the weight of your arm and hand go to the right side of your hand when you are playing with your 4th or 5th fingers.

Melancholy Waltz, beginning:

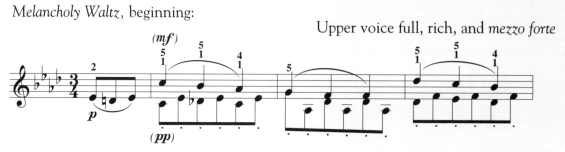

Upper voice full, rich, and *mezzo forte*

Lower voice *staccato* and *pianissimo*

When you are comfortable with your arm weight being distributed to the top of the chords, and you can control the two different dynamic levels in the same hand, then you are ready to play without making the lower voice *staccato* and can add the pedal for the full effect.

MELANCHOLY WALTZ

Franz Schubert
Op. 9 (D. 365), No. 2

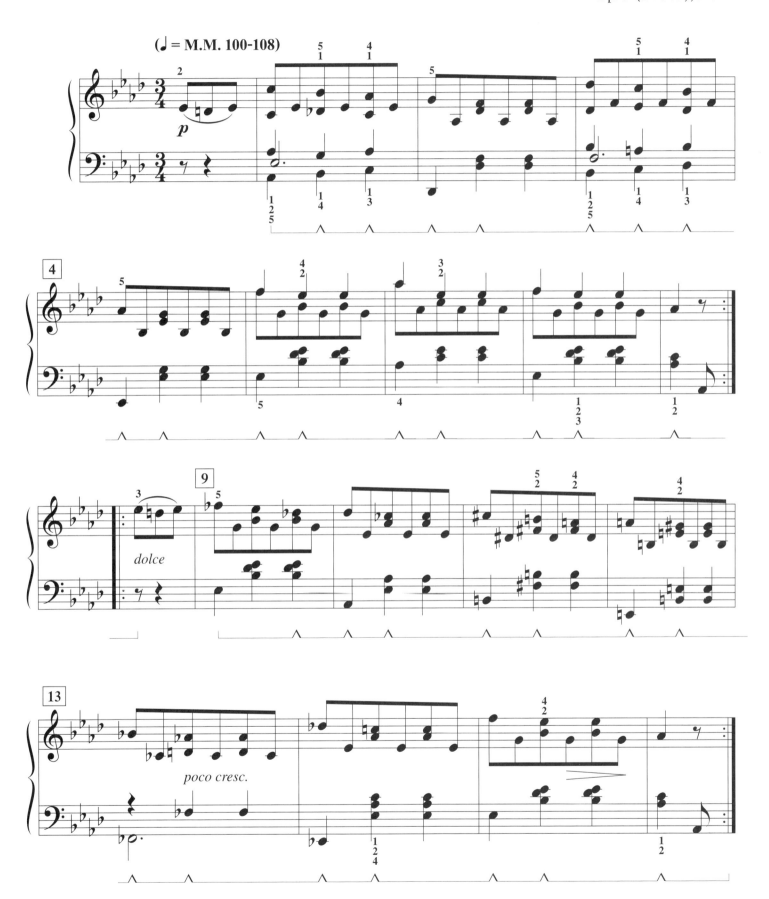

N.B. The pedaling is editorial.

FF1441

WALTZ

Franz Schubert
Op. 9 (D. 365), No. 3

N.B. The pedaling is editorial.

FF1441

WALTZ

Franz Schubert
Op. 9 (D. 365), No. 6

N.B. The pedaling, dynamics, and the *poco rit.* are editorial.

THREE DANCES

The following group of three dances, the *Ländler in A minor*, the *Valse sentimentale in A major*, and the *Valse noble in A minor*, is an example of parallel keys. All three dances may be played without separation, if desired.

The first piece in this collection, *Ländler in A minor*, was written in July of 1824, when Schubert was visiting Hungary and spending time with Caroline Esterházy, who was the youngest daughter of Count Esterházy. This piece is from a set of seventeen Ländler. A *Ländler* is a slow dance from Austria, usually in ¾ time. The same year in France, educator Louis Braille, at the age of fifteen, developed a system of raised dots enabling the blind to read.

The second piece in this set, *Valse sentimentale*, was written in the year 1823, the year that Schubert was very ill and had pressing money problems. This waltz, part of a collection of thirty-four, was written during these weeks of illness and depression. Delightful, lyrical, and sweet, this waltz was surely intended for concert performances. Waltzes are dances in triple time, slow or fast, with a strong emphasis on the first beat of every bar.

The last piece, *Valse noble*, which is from a set of twelve Valses nobles, was composed at the end of 1826, but not published until 1889. The years 1824–1826 were happy ones for Schubert, as he was enjoying a wonderful reputation as a prominent composer in Vienna. Schubert used the title "nobles" to give a feeling of elegance. These waltzes were used to accompany the dancing at domestic balls and small gatherings.

Characteristics of the Romantic Era

Listen to all three pieces on the CD recording in order to understand the feeling of the Viennese waltz. Notice the use of longer phrases in comparison with those in the Classical era. In many sections, the phrases are seamless.

Practice Strategy

Shaping phrases:

In the *Ländler*, the first phrase is eight measures long, followed by two short phrases of four measures each. Looking at the score, circle the two phrase goals in the A section. This phrase goal is the place the music naturally moves toward. Let your ear be your guide and listen to this rise of melody toward each goal. After this point, the phrase naturally tapers. Play the shorter phrases in the B section, again listening for the phrase goal.

Next listen to the *Valse sentimentale* and circle the phrase goals throughout this seamless piece. Then listen to the *Valse noble* and find the most important phrase goal, or the musical climax, of the entire piece. In which measure is it found? _____

LÄNDLER

Franz Schubert
D. 366, No. 4

N.B. The pedaling, the dynamics in measures 6 and 7, and the *poco rit.* are editorial.

Valse sentimentale

Franz Schubert
Op. 50 (D. 779), No. 13

VALSE NOBLE

from *12 Valses nobles*

Franz Schubert
Op. 77 (D. 969), No. 9

N.B. The pedaling is editorial.

TWO DANCES

Schubert wrote 452 short dances that include *waltzes, Ländler, écossaises,* and *German Dances.* The following écossaise was written on October 3, 1815, and published in 1897. On October 3, 1815, in Maryland, the city of Baltimore began construction of the nation's first monument to president George Washington. In the same year, the oldest sailing club was established in London, England, called the "Royal Yacht Squadron." The *German Dance* in this volume is part of a collection of sixteen, composed from January 1823 to July 1824.

Practice Strategy

Practicing with forward direction:

Once you have learned the notes of the *Ecossaise* on page 21 or the *German Dance* on page 22, think about the forward direction of the musical line. Apply the practice techniques discussed in the *Romantic Era, Volume One* book, and then practice larger sections to make sure that you are sustaining the line and delivering the phrases. Maintaining a continuous flow fuels the forward direction. Notice that the two phrases in each dance are eight measures long. By isolating the upper melodic line in the right hand, you will be able to hear where the phrase goals are. Singing or humming the melody and listening to the phrasing on the CD recording will also help you to understand this concept. These two pieces may be played as a set, since they demonstrate the key relationship of a third that was so popular during the Romantic era.

Ecossaise in D flat major,
measures 1–8:

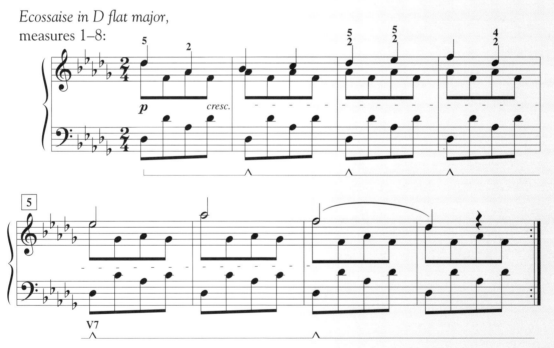

Notice that you "arrive" musically on the dominant harmony in the fifth measure, but that the phrase continues all the way until the phrase goal in the seventh measure. In the second phrase, there is a continuous flow until the very end when you reach tonic again. If you can understand and feel this musical shape, it will be much easier to play technically.

Listen to the *German Dance* and follow the same steps in order to create a forward direction in the musical phrase.

Ecossaise

Franz Schubert
D. 299, No. 5

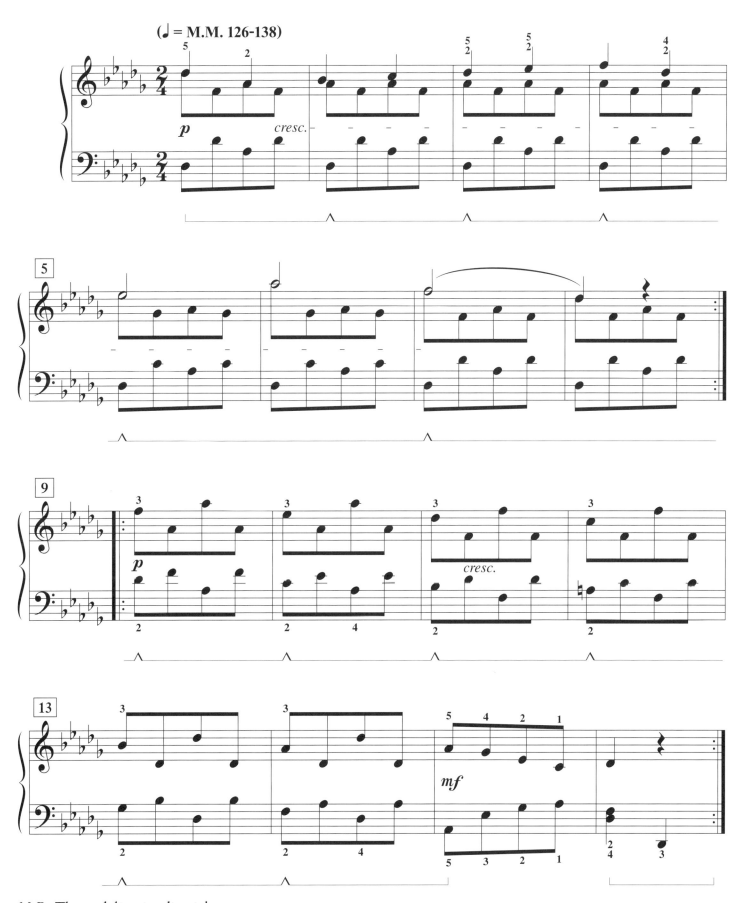

N.B. The pedaling is editorial.

GERMAN DANCE

Franz Schubert
Op. 33 (D. 783), No. 7

N.B. In the Urtext edition, *mit erhobener Dämpfung* is written at the beginning of the piece. This means to start the piece with the damper pedal already down in order to give the opening melody a warm sound.

For a smaller hand, a roll can be played in measure 15.

The slurs in measures 1, 5, 9, 10, 11, and 13 are editorial.

ROBERT SCHUMANN
(1810–1856)

Born in Zwickau, Germany, in 1810, Robert Schumann entered this world in the same year as the famous composer from Poland, Frédéric Chopin. Schumann demonstrated early ability as both pianist and composer: he took piano lessons and began composing as a young boy. In his teens, he went to Leipzig, Germany, to study law, but spent most of his time in musical and literary circles, which he found to be more interesting and more closely related to his beliefs. In time, he was able to make his family understand that it was music that he wanted to do most.

As a piano student of Friedrich Wieck, Schumann fashioned a device that he thought would "strengthen" his fingers, and instead of making him a virtuoso pianist, he lost facility in his hand. His dreams of being a concert pianist were over, but he continued to compose. His wife Clara was one of the best pianists of the time, performing Robert's compositions and her own as well. She was so highly regarded that composers would come to her to ask her advice about their compositions. You can read more about the Schumanns' marriage and children in *Succeeding with the Masters®, Romantic Era, Volume One*. When Robert and Clara were first married, in 1840, Robert wrote over 150 songs. Next he turned to orchestral music in 1841, and then to choral music in 1843. Besides these compositions, he is well known for his piano music, which is sensitive and beautiful, as you will hear in the pieces in this volume. Throughout his career, Schumann wrote symphonies, chamber music, choral music, and over 300 songs.

When Schumann was forty, his family moved to Düsseldorf for Robert's new position as the head musical director of the orchestra and chorus, presenting eight to ten concerts every year. Their move into the new community was celebrated with concerts, dinners, and an elegant ball.

Schumann wrote a great deal for the *New Journal for Music*, and his writings defined him as an expert on music during the era. He promoted new composers with his musical reviews, and discussed music education. The Schumanns became very good friends with another famous composer, Johannes Brahms, who assisted Clara and the children after Robert's death. After studying the pieces in this volume, you will be prepared to study Schumann's more advanced works, such as *Carnaval*, *Phantasiestücke*, *Scenes from Childhood*, and *Kreisleriana*.

LITTLE ROMANCE
(Kleine Romanze)

This piece from *Album for the Young* was composed with older students in mind. In the United States of America, the year after this collection was written (1849), 80,000 prospectors arrived in California in the first year of the Gold Rush.

Little Romance is an example of a *character piece*. Character pieces are short piano works that express a single mood or a programmatic idea.

Characteristics of the Romantic Era

Cantabile playing:

The melody in this piece is a duet between the soprano and the tenor voices, which may be why Schumann titled the piece as he did. The accompanimental chords could be imitating a stringed instrument. Practice by playing *only* the melodic line in the right hand, then in the left hand, and then hands together. (Therefore, you will not play the inner accompanimental chords.) *Cantabile* means to play in a "singing" style, and in order to do this, use sensitive pedaling, controlled by the ear, and listen always for a good tone. Articulate the melody by playing with flexible use of weight from your arms and hands. When you can play the melodies easily and beautifully, then it's time to add the accompaniment. Make sure it is quieter and more lugubrious.

Practice Strategy

You should feel free to use your imagination to express yourself in this music. Imagine it is a poem set to music and decide what the story line is.

Improving muscle memory:

When first learning this piece as well as any other work, be careful to always use the correct fingering so that your mind and fingers remember it. This is called "muscle memory."

Practice Strategy

The term "muscle memory" refers to how the muscles in your fingers, hands, wrists, and arms remember the feel of the keys as each note is played. Your brain sends signals to the muscles in your body to tell them how to move. If you practice in the correct way, your muscles will learn much more quickly, and you will develop technique that is reliable even when you are nervous!

In order to develop reliable muscle memory, use the following three practice strategies: unit, section, and performance.

Practice Strategy

1) Spend a little time practicing by dividing the piece into short segments — eight notes or less, or one phrase at a time. Make sure that you play with a warm and full sound, playing solidly into the keys. In order to train your fingers, this is the sound you want.

2) After unit practice, move to section practice. Place the units together to make a short section and then put two sections together to make a longer section. Practice playing

the sections straight through. By putting sections together like building blocks, eventually the sections are big enough that when you put them together you will have an entire piece! To make sure that you are playing with consistent and detailed articulations, it is important that you spend part of your practice time every day playing through sections of this piece, hands apart, preferably with the metronome.

3) In this way, section practice leads us into performance practice. Performance practice is a complete run-through of the piece. Play the piece without stopping, and then go back and identify the sections where you are having problems. Then you can create small units again and practice these repeatedly.

The Bird's Nest (*Das Vogelnest*)

LITTLE ROMANCE
(Kleine Romanze)

Robert Schumann
Op. 68, No. 19

ped. simile

ped. come prima

N.B. This pedaling is the editor's. For Urtext edition pedaling, consult the *FJH Classic Edition* of *Album for the Young*, edited by Gary Busch.

MIGNON AND LITTLE CRADLE SONG

*Mignon is a character in one of the novels by the great German writer
Johann Wolfgang von Goethe. You can still see this literary genius's home
in Frankfurt, Germany today. Mignon is a child who travels as a member
of an acrobatic troupe. Her many escapades were popular with nineteenth-
century composers, including Schumann, who wrote songs about her.
In this piece, which is one from* Album for the Young, *we can imagine
the life of a sad little girl whose daily job is to work in a circus,
balancing herself as she walks across a tightrope.*

Little Cradle Song is one of twenty short pieces written during 1832–1845 in a collection called *Albumblätter*. Schumann was living in Leipzig, Germany, at this time, where he met his future wife Clara. Elsewhere in the world, the Swiss scientist Gottfried Keller was the first to make paper from ground wood instead of from rags, and by this time in the United States 2,816 miles of railroad had been laid.

Mignon and *Little Cradle Song* are from two different collections, but there are similarities between them. One commonality is that the melody and the accompaniment are found within the same hand. Even though the texture is dense and involved, these pieces should sound delicate and fragile, and should be played with *rubato*.

**Characteristics
of the
Romantic Era**

Keeping a continuous flow:

When Clara Schumann edited *Mignon* in 1887, she wrote that the $\boldsymbol{fp}$ markings are intended merely as a slight emphasis on the final quarter note. It is easy to linger over these final beats in every measure, but instead, one must never lose sight of the overall musical line. Keep the melody flowing continuously and play to the next downbeat.

**Practice
Strategy**

The phrase shape for *Little Cradle Song* is similar. In this piece, the two-bar phrases should flow steadily to the beginning of the next phrase. When the phrases become longer (for example, in measures 7–16), it is important to create beautiful melodies from these sustained notes by creating a legato sound, even though the melodic notes cannot be connected.

Measures 1–6:

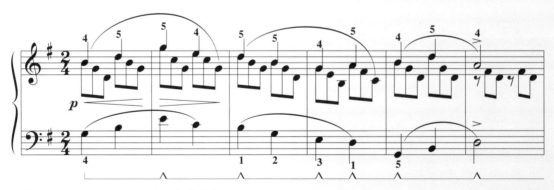

Section practice can be helpful in maintaining a melodic flow. Play a complete phrase as a section and make sure to sustain the melodic line. If a technical problem breaks the flow, break it into the unit practice discussed on pages 24 and 25. Then try the entire section again. Combining unit, section, and performance practice strategies will allow you to learn pieces very well and to perform them in a heartfelt and stylistically correct fashion.

Applying *rubato:*

Emotion is an important aspect of the music, and using rubato helps to create feeling. Make the emotion more personal when you play. Since composers during the Romantic era were interested in personal emotion, it is appropriate and expected that we use rubato in their works. Listen to the CD recording of both *Mignon* and *Little Cradle Song,* and mark directly in your score where you hear flexibility in the tempo—first a broadening, or stretching of the tempo; and then, shortly thereafter, a return back to the previous tempo.

A good marking to use for the stretching of the tempo is this:

Mignon, measures 9–12:

Rubato means to be flexible with the tempo, stretching or broadening and then pressing the tempo forward within the same phrase or shortly thereafter. The use of rubato during the Romantic era was customary.

1) Sing or hum the melody *while* you play, and you will start to realize where you can take time.

2) Sing or hum the melody *away* from the piano, and the flexible rhythm will become part of you.

3) Practice either *Mignon* or *Little Cradle Song* with a steady tempo, without any rubato. Instead, play it with the metronome, around ♩ = 72. Then, turn off the metronome and add a beautiful rubato. It is important to have the appropriate amount of rubato—too much or too little can spoil the shape of the individual phrases and the piece as a whole.

It is important to be able to play the piece in time with the metronome, so that you can control your rubato. The rubato only works if you have established a clear and steady tempo to stretch or push against.

Mignon can be found on pages 30 and 31, *Little Cradle Song* on pages 32 and 33.

MIGNON

Robert Schumann
Op. 68, No. 35

Langsam, zart (slowly, delicately) (♩ = M.M. 80)

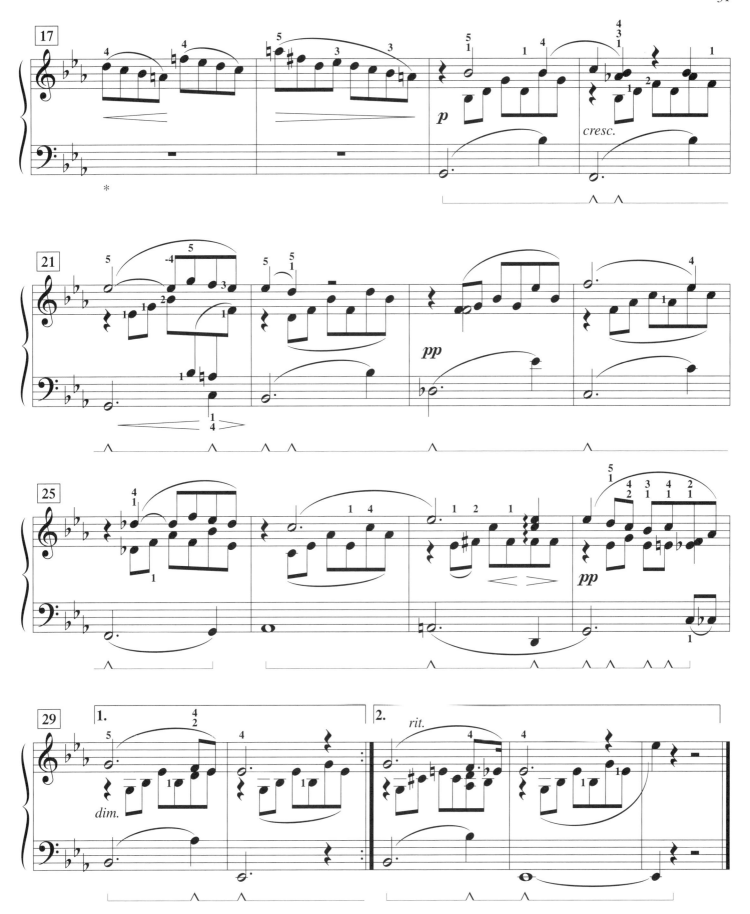

N.B. This pedaling is the editor's. For Urtext edition pedaling, consult the *FJH Classic Edition* of *Album for the Young*, edited by Gary Busch.

*Measures 17–19 can be quarter and "flutter pedaled" since modern pianos are more resonant than those in Schumann's period.

LITTLE CRADLE SONG
(Wiegenliedchen)

Robert Schumann
Op. 124, No. 6

Nicht schnell (not fast) (♩ = ca. 88)

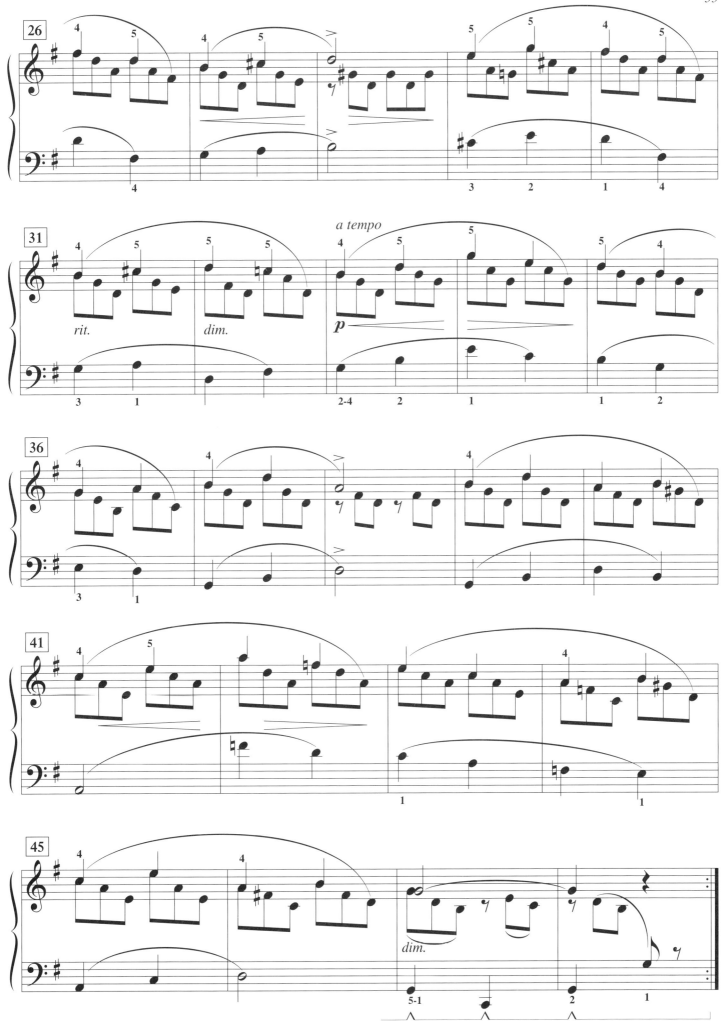

33

N.B. The pedaling is editorial.

FF1441

ST. NICHOLAS
(Knecht Ruprecht)

This piece tells the story of the nineteenth-century German equivalent of America's Jolly Old St. Nicholas. St. Nicholas gave to the good children, but disciplined the bad children by giving them lumps of coal.

Drama as an essential element of romantic literature:

Characteristics of the Romantic Era

Listening to the CD recording of this piece, mark directly in your score the ternary ABA form. Can you imagine St. Nicholas clattering on the stairs when you hear the fiery trills and the diminished chords in measures 9 to 16?

Measures 9–16:

In the B section (in F major and then in D flat major), what do you imagine is the scene with St. Nicholas? Is he giving gifts to the children who have been good? What else could he be doing in the house at this time?

Practice Strategy

Contrast in music creates drama:

In order to create a convincing portrayal of St. Nicholas, plan with your teacher how you will create contrast between the A and B sections. The sound, imagery, and emotion should be completely different. Playing the B section with a lighter touch can be a good way to help change the character.

St. Nicholas
Courtesy of St. Nicholas Center,
www.stnicholascenter.org

ST. NICHOLAS
(Knecht Ruprecht)

Robert Schumann
Op. 68, No. 12

N.B. Half pedal or quarter pedal measures 25-48.

*Pedaling and fingering are the same as before.

N.B. Pedaling is the editor's.

THE PIANO DURING THE ROMANTIC ERA

The piano in the Romantic era was a very different instrument from the keyboard instruments of the Baroque and Classical eras, since the new piano was capable of producing a wide dynamic range and greater control. The piano went through many modifications in the second half of the 1800's, until it became essentially the piano that we know today. The new piano construction methods and the resulting expanded capabilities gave the piano new qualities that affected the way composers approached and wrote for the instrument. The piano strings and frame were greatly enhanced from those of Beethoven's day, now giving pianists greater range of tone color and dynamics. Developments with the soundboards increased the resonance and sustaining capabilities of the instrument, and this feature helped to prolong the tone, making the piano "sing." The knee pedals of the Classical era gave way to the foot pedals we use today. As the damper pedal improved, pianists were able to play with more of a *legato* sound, and harmonies could be blended together beautifully.

For the first time, pianos were turned sideways on stage so that the audience could see the pianist's profile during a performance. This was the age of the virtuoso, and it was important for audiences to be able to see the pianist play during concerts. The piano became the center of activity in the home. Every evening families and friends would get together to sing with the piano, listen to each other play solo piano music, and play chamber music with piano. In fact, playing the piano became one of the most popular forms of recreation during the nineteenth century. It was important for young ladies to learn how to play the instrument, since they would be expected to play at social events. The best pianists of the day were considered heroes! When music was composed for orchestras and operas, it was immediately arranged for solo piano or piano duet, and this is why so many people knew all of the music of the day. For instance, all of the Beethoven symphonies could be played in one's living room with a friend! More music was published for piano than for any other instrument or ensemble. By 1847, there were 180 piano makers in Paris alone, and 300 in England. The majority of the music published at that time in Europe was for the piano, and piano manufacturing was the largest industry in the United States.

Pianos were often extremely ornate:

Chopin's favorite piano was the Pleyel piano, pictured above
Courtesy of Period Piano Company

LITTLE HUNTING SONG
(Jägerliedchen)

This piece, from Schumann's *Album for the Young*, was composed in 1848. Along with five other pieces, Schumann composed this one for his oldest daughter Marie, and gave it to her as a present on her seventh birthday. *Album for the Young* has forty-three pieces, and often references the family life Robert and Clara shared with their seven children. Clara taught the easier pieces to their children, and we can assume that she played the more difficult works for the family to enjoy.

An example of a programmatic piece:

The romantic composers, writers, and visual artists viewed the forest and countryside as a place for adventure and mystery, and pieces that depicted hunting were popular. This programmatic piece creates an image in the mind of the listener that relates to the title.

Characteristics of the Romantic Era

Strong sense of rhythm helping to define a piece:

This compound-meter piece should be played with exuberance. Perhaps you can imagine horses galloping when you hear the eighth notes. You can hear the hunting horns call with open intervals of fourths in measures one and two. In what other measures can you hear the hunting calls?

From the upbeat to measure 17 through 21, we can imagine an animal or bird being chased:

Practice Strategy

The drama and excitement of this piece will be evident if you keep a steady tempo throughout the work. Counting aloud while you play is one of the most helpful practice strategies to accomplish this. Even though it requires extra concentration, it will be well worth the effort and will produce results in your playing. After counting aloud, try making an accent with your voice on the major beats while you play. Counting aloud will help keep you from rushing, while still feeling the forward direction of the musical line. Practicing this piece with accurate rhythm, first slowly so that you play the correct notes and rhythms and then up to tempo, will allow you to add the dynamics, articulations, and pedaling that are so important in bringing this piece to life.

LITTLE HUNTING SONG
(*Jägerliedchen*)

Robert Schumann
Op. 68, No. 7

N.B. The pedaling is Schumann's except for measures 21 to the end.

The First Railroad-Car, 1825

FF1441

THE HORSEMAN
(Reiterstück)

Characteristics of the Romantic Era

Practice Strategy

This piece, like many pieces in this era, is programmatic, which means that it tells a story or creates an image in the mind. Thinking about the title of this piece and listening and looking at the music, can you see why Schumann named it The Horseman?

Creating the mood of the piece for a successful performance:

When hearing this programmatic piece, it is easy to imagine the scene of a rider and his horse at night. The constant pulse of the duple compound meter suggests the sound of a galloping horse. Cultivating a good sense of rhythm will carry you in the study and performance of this piece.

There are three main sections to this work:
The horseman's approach—measures 1–8
His deafening presence—measures 9–16
His gradual retreat into the distance—measures 17–54

In order to create this mood, one must play evenly and rhythmically:

1) With the metronome set to a comfortable tempo, play and count aloud, subdividing the sixteenth notes like this:

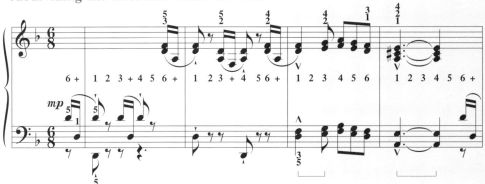

This will keep you from rushing, while still feeling the forward direction of the line.

2) On the first two notes of every three-note motive, move your wrist by freely dropping it below your knuckle bridge. On the last beat of the motive, roll up on your fingertips moving toward the fallboard, and let your wrists follow the line of motion. This motion is not too large or exaggerated, but natural. Once this gesture becomes effortless, you will feel a flowing rhythmic pulse. Listen carefully to yourself play all of the sixteenth notes clearly, and try not to tense your muscles!

Finding places to relax for better facility:

This piece needs to sound dramatic and mysterious. It is necessary for you to have some tension in your muscles while you play, but it is crucial to learn how and when to release this tension. There are places in the music where you should make yourself aware of the importance of relaxing your arms and wrists. To practice, play a phrase, and then incorporate a release/lift motion into the piece without changing the tempo. Ultimately, you will execute this motion quickly, but it will give your muscles a tiny moment to relax. There are three places on the first page where large chords are played at the ends of phrases, and it is here where you will *drop* your arm weight instead in order to relax. Listen to the practice strategy on the CD as a guide, because it will help you become aware of the need for tension and relaxation in the same muscles.

THE HORSEMAN
(Reiterstück)

Robert Schumann
Op. 68, No. 23

Kurz und bestimmt (short and very clear) (♩. = M.M. 100)

46

FF1441

N.B. The slurs and pedal indications are editorial except for the pedal markings in measures 31–33.

SOLITARY FLOWERS
(Einsame Blumen)

This piece is from *Forest Scenes (Waldszenen)*, composed during 1848 and 1849. This was the time that the Schumanns moved to Dresden, Germany, and Robert was inspired to write many famous works, such as the *Piano Concerto in A minor*. Revolutionary uprisings in the city caused the family to move on to Düsseldorf in 1850.

Practice Strategy

Playing seamlessly:

Solitary Flowers is a splendid example of the poetry in music that was prevalent during the era. For the performer, the challenge is to carefully balance the two lines within the same hand, and make it sound easy! This seamless writing can be equated to a string of pearls. Each beautiful pearl follows the prior one—so, too, do the notes that create each phrase of this piece.

Compare measures 32 to 37 with measures 1 to 7. What makes this repetitive material different?
(Check all those below that apply.)
_____ Different left-hand harmony
_____ The rhythm has changed
_____ More voices have been added

Can you find the measure where the soprano and alto voices have switched?

Think about each phrase being very long, and let your ear be your guide as to where the phrase goals are within each phrase. Notice that the first resting place in this piece is after measure 10.

Practice Strategy

Keen listening:

The simplicity of this piece makes it intimate and beautiful. To create a magical sound, listen while you play, to be sure that your left-hand and your right-hand notes are played exactly at the same time. If one hand comes in early or late, even for a split second, the magic is lost because the clarity of the texture is muddied. Listen to the practice strategy on the CD recording to hear examples of how the piece should sound, and examples of how it should *not* sound!

It is very important that the rhythm in the two hands line up perfectly. If it does, you will create an enchanting sound as the melody and accompaniment float along perfectly together.

SOLITARY FLOWERS
(Einsame Blumen)

Robert Schumann
Op. 82, No. 3

N.B. The pedal markings in this piece are the only ones Schumann provided.
However, pedal should be used throughout.

EVENING SONG
(Abendlied)

This lovely movement is from *Sonata for the Young, No. 2*, composed in 1853. Schumann wrote three sonatas for young people and dedicated them to his three daughters. The first sonata is dedicated to Julie, the second to Elisa, and the third to Marie.

Characteristics of the Romantic Era

Most of the romantic composers were interested in nature, in the fantastic, and above all, in emotional expression.

Schumann co-founded a newspaper, the *New Journal for Music (Neue Zeitschrift für Musik)*, which became one of the most influential music journals of the time, and many of his published writings were found there. He would sign the articles he wrote with different names, depending on the mood of the article. The various names he used depicted imaginary figures in Schumann's mind that he felt were different facets of his own personality. His favorite two imaginary people, Florestan and Eusebius, had opposite personalities—Florestan was outgoing and energetic, while Eusebius was an introvert and poet. As you listen to *Evening Song*, which personality would you say influenced this piece?

Practice Strategy

Shaping phrases:

This beautiful piece needs to be phrased carefully in order to achieve the optimal effect. Each phrase is short, and one must shape several of these shorter phrases into longer musical phrases. Notice that there are few resting places in this music, and one should always feel the forward direction of the musical line.

Measures 1–6:

Practice Strategy

The *espressivo* (*fp*) dynamic markings are an important way of emphasizing emotion in the music. When you see this marking, press into the key, giving it more emphasis and special weight than the other notes within the same phrase, but without giving it a sharp accent. Play it with tenderness, emotion, and extra warmth. The marking may not only indicate a change in dynamic, but also a stretching of the tempo at this point. The extra time can help to emphasize that note without forcing it. Be sure to make the first note of the other phrases quiet, however, in order to have a place from which to start dynamically.

Picture of the Beloved
German, 19th century

EVENING SONG
(Abendlied)

Robert Schumann
Op. 118, No. 2

Langsam (slowly) (♩ = M.M. 50)

N.B. The pedaling is editorial.

PETER TCHAIKOVSKY

(1840–1893)

Pyotr (Peter) Ilyich Tchaikovsky was born on May 7, 1840, in Russia. He is known for writing some of the most popular classical pieces in the history of Western music. Born in Votkinsk, in the district of Viatka, Tchaikovsky did not come from a musical family. When he was young, his mother took him to see an opera by Mikhail Glinka, who is considered to be the "father of Russian music." This experience changed young Peter's life. Glinka influenced many great Russian composers besides Tchaikovsky, such as Balakirev, Rimsky-Korsakov, Mussorgsky, Borodin, Stravinsky, and Prokofiev.

Tchaikovsky's mother died when he was only fourteen. Like Schumann, Tchaikovsky attended law school but knew that his heart was for music. After completing a law degree, Tchaikovsky studied at the Conservatory of Music in St. Petersburg, where he was such an excellent student and composer that he became a professor at the Moscow Conservatory when he was only twenty-six. From 1868 to 1874, in addition to teaching he wrote reviews of music for Moscow newspapers.

Tchaikovsky began a correspondence and friendship with a woman by the name of Nadezhda von Meck. She was a wealthy widow who played a very important role in his life. She was a great lover of nature and music, and although she had eleven children, she led a secluded existence by her own choice. When she learned of Tchaikovsky's financial difficulties, she paid him to write compositions for large fees. Every month, she sent Pyotr a check so that he could spend more time composing. For thirteen years they corresponded, yet they never met! Tchaikovsky felt that "one should not see one's guardian angel in the flesh."[1] Once they were in the same city at the same time, but he declined the opportunity to meet her.

From 1877 to 1878, Tchaikovsky traveled to Italy, Switzerland, Paris, and Vienna for concerts of his music. He dedicated his fourth epic symphony to his patron and friend, von Meck. From February to October of 1878, his *Children's Album* was composed, and all of the pieces in this collection except one are from this album.

A group of Russian composers—Balakirev, Borodin, Rimsky-Korsakov, Mussorgsky, and Cui—were called the "Russian Five." They wrote strongly nationalistic works which were very patriotic and Russian. Their music has a heroic character, with beautiful melodies influenced by folk melodies, harmonies, and rhythms. Even though Tchaikovsky was influenced by his native Russia, he gravitated instead toward the European romantic style. When you play Tchaikovsky's piano pieces in this book, you can decide for yourself whether they sound nationalistic. Some of Tchaikovsky's most famous pieces are the ballets *The Nutcracker* (1892), *Swan Lake* (1876), *Romeo and Juliet* (1869, revised in 1870 and 1880), and *Sleeping Beauty* (1889). The *1812 Overture* and his symphonies also show his use of keen rhythms and a nostalgic character. When his *Piano Concerto No. 1* had its world premiere in Boston in 1875, critics wrote that it was "unplayable." Critics also attacked his violin concerto, but it, as well as the piano concerto, are now two of his most celebrated works. His last symphony, the *Pathétique*, was composed in 1893, the last year of his life.

[1] Laura Kuhn, ed., *Baker's Biographical Dictionary of Musicians* (New York: Schirmer Books, 2001), p. 3598.

MAZURKA

Tchaikovsky began to write this *mazurka*, which is part of his *Children's Album*, in 1878. The year before, Thomas Edison had invented the phonograph, and in 1878 he produced it commercially. A mazurka is a Polish dance that has strong beats not only on the downbeats, but also on other beats in the measure. When you listen to the piece on the CD, notice on which beats the accents fall.

In the Romantic era, a strong sense of tonic to dominant movement in the harmony still exists. However, the harmonic language is expanded for added color and emphasizes not only tonic, subdominant, and dominant chords, but also chords that are outside of the tonic key.

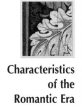

Characteristics of the Romantic Era

Mark the ternary form directly in your score. In the A section, the phrases begin on the downbeat, while in the B section, the melodic phrases begin on the upbeat. Where does the B section begin? _____ Where is the return of the A (A^1) section?
_____

Playing dotted rhythms:

This piece will be effective if the dotted rhythms are accurate. The following sixteenth-note rhythmic pattern is found throughout this piece.

Practice Strategy

Measures 1–4:

With the metronome set at ♩ = 76, count aloud while playing the piece, as shown in the musical example above. Subdividing each beat clearly, while counting aloud, will allow you to play with the accurate rhythm. Be aware of your playing, so as not to let these rhythmic patterns turn into a triplet pattern, like this:

Practice at various speeds while continuously subdividing in order to be completely successful!

Mazurka

Pyotr Ilyich Tchaikovsky
Op. 39, No. 11

Not very fast (mazurka tempo) (♩ = ca. 116)

N.B. The pedaling is editorial.

Neapolitan Song

In Tchaikovsky's *Children's Album,* he included a German, a French, and an Italian folk song. Some romantic composers used the rhythms and melodies of foreign countries in order to evoke the color and atmosphere of that country. This is called *exoticism.*

Characteristics of the Romantic Era

Practice Strategy

Playing rapid staccato notes in the left hand:

In order to avoid feeling fatigue in the left hand while playing repetitive chords, try the following practice strategy. Drop your arm weight on every downbeat, and then for the repeated chords that follow, focus on letting your wrist be at a different height for each chord. Start with a lower wrist for the first chord. For the second chord, let your wrist move so that it is parallel to the floor, and then for the third chord, your wrist should be slightly higher again. This practice strategy should be practiced very slowly in order to remember exactly where your wrist should be, and then you can work your speed up until you can play it *a tempo.* Play on the tips of your fingers, and you will not get tired!

Practice Strategy

"Follow the leader":

Sometimes pianists get so focused on the right hand that they forget what is going on in the left hand. Let your left hand be the leader, and have your right hand follow it. Imagine that your left hand is the more important hand, and remember that the music of the left hand is what drives the rhythm and gives energy to the entire piece.

Practice sections of the piece, bringing out the left-hand part. You can sing or count out loud, and imagine that a stringed instrument is playing the left-hand part and a happy person from Naples, Italy, is singing the melody. First, play the left hand alone. Make it crisp and even, accenting the second beat. Then add the right hand, still feeling that your left hand is in command.

Measures 1–5:

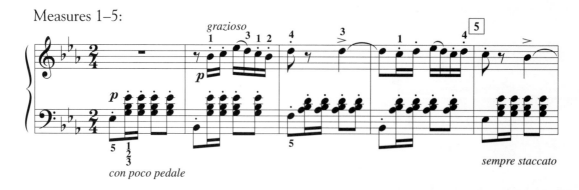

With this practice strategy you will gain confidence, and the rhythmic vitality of the work will become evident. You will also find that you will not rush during a performance!

Neapolitan Song

Pyotr Ilyich Tchaikovsky
Op. 39, No. 18

sempre staccato la mano sinistra

62

FF1441

N.B. The pedaling is editorial, as well as the dynamics in measures 41, 43, 44, 48, and 51.

Sweet Dream

This piece is also part of *Children's Album.* In 1878, the year the collection was composed, the United States began to manufacture bicycles, and people used typewriters instead of our modern computers.

**Characteristics
of the
Romantic Era**

In this piece, Tchaikovsky blends characteristics of the Classical era with characteristics of the Romantic era. As in the Classical era, Tchaikovsky uses a traditional form. This piece has three sections, which makes it an ABA ternary form. What makes the B section different from the A sections? _____ The emotion expressed in this piece is highly personal, and this is a romantic trait.

**Practice
Strategy**

Balancing melody with accompaniment:

In the A section of this lovely piece, we see the melody in the right hand against a moving bass line and inner accompaniment in the left hand:

Here are three ways to practice the A section:

1) Play only the melody and the moving bass line, without pedal, in order to concentrate on the fingering and listen to the balance of the voices.

2) Practice only the left hand, slowly and accurately, in order to make the inner accompaniment light and even. Enjoy playing these offbeats along with the moving bass line, balancing the melodic line over the accompaniment part. You may add pedal if you wish.

3) Only when you are secure and comfortable with these two practice strategies should you practice all three parts at once.

In the B section, the left hand now has the melody. Since the melody is heard around middle C and below, less pedal is needed in order to keep the melodic line pure and beautiful. In measure 22, when the right hand joins the left hand in playing the melody, pedal may be added again for more resonance.

Measures 21–24:

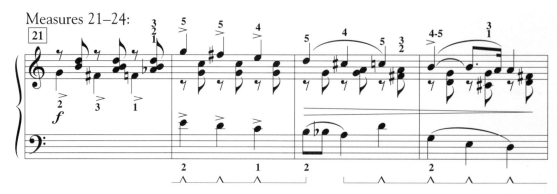

Sweet Dream

Pyotr Ilyich Tchaikovsky
Op. 39, No. 21

66

FF1441

Two women during the Romantic era, 1857

THE LARK'S SONG

Characteristics of the Romantic Era

Another piece from *Children's Album*, *The Lark's Song*, exemplifies the romantic notion of the importance of nature. Differing from the Baroque and Classical eras, Romantic-era composers, artists, and writers spent time in nature and made it an essential part of their imaginative thought process.

Practice Strategy

Playing with a supple wrist:

Listen to this piece—can you imagine a graceful bird singing? A sure way to achieve the mood and style is to practice with a supple wrist, and to be sure to breathe at the ends of the longer phrases in order to keep you from rushing.

The places where you can lift your wrist for a clear and clean ending are at the end of every slur, and for eighth-note chords in the left hand.

Measures 1 and 2:

Measures 11–13:

You might find it beneficial to mark the places in your music where you will lift your wrists. This technical approach of lifting, or releasing your wrists quickly, will help you create a convincing performance. This release of the wrist creates the crisp, *staccato* sound that you want; it will help give the ends of the short phrases a feeling of needed space; it will give your upper body a moment to relax its muscles, and it's the best way to be ready for the next phrase. Listen to the practice strategy on the recording to further understand this concept. Experimenting with this strategy will help you to convey the lively spirit of the piece.

Practice Strategy

How to play a piece faster:

When you are ready to play this piece more quickly, remember "lighter means faster." This means if you can lighten your touch throughout, you will be able to play it more quickly without any trouble. Just remember that it still must be even. You can refer to the three practice strategies (unit, section, and performance) on pages 24 and 25 for further help.

A farm during the Romantic era
German, 19th century

THE LARK'S SONG

Pyotr Ilyich Tchaikovsky
Op. 39, No. 22

con poco pedale

CHANSON TRISTE
(Sad Song)

Two years before this piece was written, in 1876, the telephone was invented
by Alexander Graham Bell; in 1879, the year after this piece was written,
Thomas Edison invented the light bulb.

**Practice
Strategy**

Interpreting a phrase:

Notice that many of the phrases have a repeated upper melodic note. There are several
ways you can phrase this melodic line.

1) *Crescendo* to the next downbeat, like this:

2) Make a *diminuendo* and then a *crescendo*:

3) Place a slight emphasis on the first
   and third beats of the measure:

You and your teacher can decide which phrasing you like best and for which sections of
the piece. (Listening to the performance track will also help you in your interpretation.)

Voicing the melody using two hands:

**Practice
Strategy**

Remember that to "voice" a melody means to bring out one of the voices in an interval
or chord that is played *within the same hand*. The following practice strategy will help you
to learn how to voice.

Play each beat very slowly, and play the top melodic line with your right hand and the
inner chords in the treble clef with your left hand. Make all of the voice's tones full, rich,
and warm, but bring out the melody more. This is just another way to hear the music and
be focused on the musicality of each phrase.

Measures 1–4:

CHANSON TRISTE
(Sad Song)

Pyotr Ilyich Tchaikovsky
Op. 40, No. 2

Allegro non troppo (♩ = ca. 104)
la melodia con molto espressione

74

FRÉDÉRIC CHOPIN

(1810–1849)

 Frédéric François Chopin was born in Poland. His French father was a schoolteacher, and his Polish mother was a woman of culture and refinement. The family lived in Warsaw. Frédéric took piano lessons, studying the works of J.S. Bach, Haydn, Mozart, and Beethoven, and gave his first public recital in Warsaw at the age of eight. When he was sixteen years old, he entered the music conservatory, having already composed piano music under the titles of *mazurkas, polonaises,* and *rondos.* He studied there for three years.

The piano was Chopin's favorite instrument. He is the only great composer in history who wrote almost exclusively for it. Imagine having one thing in life that makes you happy, and being so devoted to it! It is said that Chopin composed while improvising at the piano, and when you hear his music, you might agree.

When Chopin was eighteen, he started to play solo concerts in Warsaw and in Vienna, and the critics loved him. When he was only twenty-one, Chopin moved to Paris, where more opportunities were available to him in his chosen career of music. In Paris he became friends with famous musicians—Franz Liszt, one of the greatest pianists of all time, as well as the best pianists of the day, Frédéric Kalkbrenner and Ignace Pleyel. All of his fellow musicians admired Chopin's compositions, as well as his playing. Robert Schumann met Chopin, and was most kind towards him. Frédéric quickly established himself as a performer and teacher among the members of high society.

From 1828 to 1832, between the ages of eighteen and twenty-two, Chopin concertized and wrote brilliant showpieces for the piano. He also composed concertos, which are virtuosic pieces for piano and orchestra. He taught many students, and wrote études and many other kinds of pieces for them. Some of his students wrote books about what it was like to study with the great master, so that today we can learn what Chopin was like as a teacher.

In 1837 Liszt introduced Chopin to the novelist George Sand, a woman of forceful personality, who valued the independence and the freedoms that came readily to men. Theirs became an important relationship, and they were together for eight years before they parted, at times living at Nohant, her serene chateau in central France, or traveling to the island of Mallorca to compose and write, thinking that the weather there would help Chopin's frail health. Instead, weather conditions were harsh, and Chopin's health suffered. Chopin refined his twenty-four preludes in Mallorca.

When Chopin died, 3,000 mourners came to his funeral to pay their respects. During his lifetime he wrote fifty-eight mazurkas, twenty nocturnes, fifteen polonaises, seventeen waltzes, four ballades, twenty-five preludes (the first twenty-four were published in 1839 and the last one, in C-sharp minor, was published in 1841), twenty-seven studies, four impromptus, four scherzos, three rondos, two sonatas, and various other large-scale works that pianists play regularly. His piano music is innovative, distinctive, and very beautiful, and his works influenced many famous composers who followed him. To this day he is remembered for his good looks, frail health, sensitive playing, and chivalrous manner.

to Émile Gaillard

SOSTENUTO
(Feuille d'Album)

Émile Gaillard, to whom this piece was dedicated, was a banker, friend, and student of Chopin. In addition to this piece, Chopin also dedicated his unnumbered *Mazurka in A minor* of 1841 to Gaillard. Only two men received dedications by Chopin—all the rest were dedicated to women. This piece, which was written on July 20, 1840, stayed in the possession of Gaillard's family until it was finally published in the mid-twentieth century.

During the Romantic era, composers expressed phrases in varying lengths. Notice how this works in this piece:

The first two phrases are short phrases:

Characteristics of the Romantic Era

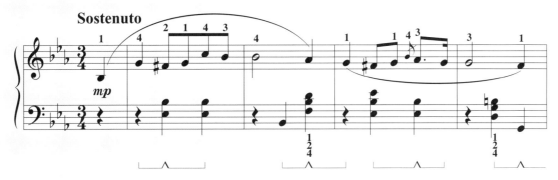

Notice that the third phrase, a four-measure phrase, is much longer. The first two phrases lead to the long phrase and make perfect musical sense. Listening to the piece, notice where all of the other "short-short-long" phrasing occurs and mark it in your score.

Applying *rubato*:

This piece will be lovely, if played with *rubato*. Listen to the CD recording and hear how the tempo slows and then returns to the previous tempo with great fluidity. Practice the entire piece with the metronome, without any tempo fluctuations, and then turn off the metronome and sing along with the sad melody. One needs to have a strong rhythmic sense first, and then add rubato, which pulls and pushes against the basic tempo without destroying it. Pushing or pulling against the tempo, while maintaining the overall sense of pulse and direction, can emphasize the emotional quality of this romantic music.

Practice Strategy

The importance of hands-alone practice:

To make sure you are playing with consistent and correct phrasing, it is important that you spend part of your practice time every day playing through sections of this piece, hands apart, preferably with the metronome. Listen for the beauty in each phrase. Practice at a slow speed, and then increase your tempo. Then play the piece hands together, focusing on the left hand instead of the right hand, and you will notice that your playing will be more confident and accurate.

Practice Strategy

to Émile Gaillard
SOSTENUTO
(Feville d'Ablum)

Frédéric Chopin
KK IVb/10

N.B. The pedaling is editorial. Grace notes should be played on the beat.

THREE PRELUDES

Chopin's friend Ignace Pleyel liked Chopin's *Twenty-four Preludes* very much, and gave him the money to have them published. Most of the preludes were composed before Chopin's trip to the island of Mallorca, which he took to help his deteriorating health. Mallorca is the largest of the Balearic Islands, off the coast of Spain, and has emerald-green mountains and palm trees. Unfortunately, instead of being sunny and warm, it was windy and rainy there. During his stay in Mallorca, Chopin selected and polished the preludes for publishing.

The preludes appeared in print in 1839, the year before the world's first postage stamp was issued in Britain. Robert Schumann wrote of the preludes,

> …I must signalize them as most remarkable. I will confess I expected
> something quite different, carried out in the grand style of his studies.
> It is almost the contrary here; these are sketches, the beginning of studies,
> or, if you will, ruins, eagles' feathers, all strangely intermingled. One recognizes
> Chopin in his pauses, in his impetuous respiration. He is the boldest, the
> proudest poet soul of his time.[1]

Characteristics of the Romantic Era

Practice Strategy

Emotion is a strong aspect of the music:

You will find three of Chopin's preludes in this volume. The *Prelude in B minor*, No. 6 is a mood picture. It is a study in control, with the right-hand repetitive gesture setting the mood. This gesture should be constantly present in your mind, even though it is not the melody. This prelude is intimate, subjective, and sad. Chopin indicated pedal only in measures 13, 14, and 23. However, this piece is usually heard with pedaling in every measure. The Pleyel pianos, Chopin's favorite, had a very different resonance and volume range than our modern-day piano; so, the pedaling was very different in Chopin's day.

The *Prelude in A major*, No. 7 seems like a short sketch based on the Polish national dance, the mazurka. This prelude should be played with innocent simplicity because of its regular phrasing and form. Make sure that all of the notes of every chord are played exactly together for clarity. There is only one point of departure from the regular form, and this is found in measure 12. This musical climax must be special. Use *rubato* in measure 11 so that you can prepare the chord in measure 12. This chord will be the warmest, loudest chord in the piece. Play it within the context of the rest of the piece's dynamic level, however, so that it will be elegant and beautiful. You will notice that most of Chopin's pedaling stretches through bar lines, and if the piece is played quietly and sweetly, the blurring of tones over the bass note will be quite effective. Listen to the CD recording to see how the pianist modifies Chopin's pedaling.

The *Prelude in C minor*, No. 20 is a sorrowful sketch that sounds like a funeral march. Perhaps Chopin was thinking of his own illness when he wrote this dramatic piece. Chopin added pedal only at the very end. However, the need for pedal is so obvious on every chord change that Chopin simply just left it out. It was not uncommon for many composers of the Romantic era to leave out markings, since they trusted the musicians of the day to know the style and play appropriately.

Creating your own interpretation through listening:

Practice Strategy

Find two recordings of the famous preludes by Chopin. Listen to the first recording and mark directly in your score with a colored pencil everything that you hear the pianist do. Mark in all of the phrasing, the dynamics, the places where *rubato* was used, and anything else that was special to this particular pianist. Then take another colored pencil, and mark in the interpretation of the second pianist. Lastly, do the same with the interpretation on the CD in the book. Write the name of the pianists in the respective colors at the top of each prelude in order to remember each interpretation, and also include what tempo each pianist chose. Do you notice how different the three interpretations are and how they are similar? As you come to master the basics and become more familiar with the romantic style, you too can engage yourself in creating a personal interpretation of the music.

[1] James Huneker, ed., <u>Chopin</u>: The Man and His Music (New York: Dover Publications, 1966), p. 120.

View of a Polish Village with Peasants' Cottages
By Jan Piotr Norblin

PRELUDE

Frédéric Chopin
Op. 28, No. 7

N.B. The pedaling is Chopin's.

In measure 12, the five lowest notes may be rolled with the left hand if played by a smaller hand.

PRELUDE

Frédéric Chopin
Op. 28, No. 20

FF1441

Prelude

Frédéric Chopin
Op. 28, No. 6

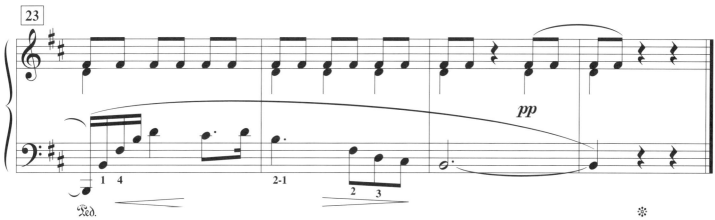

N.B. The 𝕻𝕰𝖉. ✻ are Chopin's only pedal markings in this piece.

CANTABILE

Students of Chopin documented Chopin's teaching as well as his playing. It was written that Chopin played with complete control and used many shadings of *pianissimo*. He could play many passages ever so softly and delicately, with a wonderful sense of balance and symmetry. It is interesting to note that Chopin did not like to play publicly, but rather preferred playing in salons for small audiences. This piece was written in 1834, two years before the *Arc de Triomphe* (*Arch of Triumph*) was completed in Paris.

**Practice
Strategy**

The importance of a *singing legato*:

This piece, as well as many other romantic works, must be played with a singing legato sound. Chopin believed that in order to play his music well, one should listen to great singers, so pianists could truly learn what a singing legato is. To achieve this sustained, beautiful sound, use the upper arm in addition to the hand, wrist, and fingers. Playing with a supple arm and wrist, follow the curves of Chopin's music. For example, when a note is followed by a wide leap up, move your wrist to the right and then play the next note with a rich and warm tone. Let your elbow move with your wrist. Remember that the shape of the line guides the shape of your arm motion. The singing legato from the first note to the second needs your concentration in order to master it. Drop deeply into the key and then slowly move your elbow slightly away from your body. When you are playing on your fingertip, release the key and play the D again, this time with the fifth finger:

When you see a passage such as the following one, follow the curves of the music again with your wrist in order to create an elasticity of phrasing without any halts, stumbles, or explosive dynamics. Chopin's melodic line in this piece and others should be performed in a flowing, circular manner, and never square.

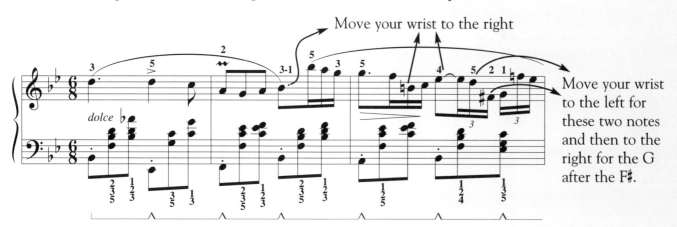

Move your wrist to the right

Move your wrist to the left for these two notes and then to the right for the G after the F♯.

Enjoy every melodic phrase and sing it to understand its musical shape. Develop your own palette of colors and different dynamics—using the pedal—to shape each phrase and make the melody sing. The left hand, even though it plays chords, can be shaped so that it sounds as though it is played in a *legato* manner. Practice the left hand slowly, and let your wrist and arm be at a different location on the keyboard for each chord. For example, the second beat B-flat major chord will be played with the fingers and the hand in the middle of the keys, while the third beat, the B-flat seventh chord, will be played with the fingers and the hand up into the keys, close to the fallboard of the piano. If you can concentrate on the placement of your hand and fingers for each chord, then you will not have to reach for any notes. Lift your wrist and play on your fingertips after every third beat to relax your arm.

The Arch of Triumph in Paris, France, commissioned by Napoleon and completed in 1836
Courtesy of Helen Marlais

Frédéric Chopin.

Encore un beau nom à inscrire dans ce triste nécrologe où tant d'artistes ont trouvé place, alors que leur vie semblait à peine à son commencement. — Frédéric Chopin était né en 1810, à Zelazowawola, près de Varsovie. Son premier maître de piano fut un vieux Bohême, nommé Zywni. Mais il ne tarda pas à être en état de diriger seul ses études pour cet instrument. Les seules leçons qu'il prit dès lors consistèrent à visiter les principales villes musicales de l'Allemagne pour y entendre les artistes les plus célèbres. Pénétré de leurs exemples, en même temps que poussé par une irrésistible individualité, il revenait, après les avoir entendus, se renfermer chez lui, et là, solitaire, rêveur, méditant ses premières impressions, recueillant tous ses frais souvenirs, comparant entre eux les plus parfaits modèles de son art, afin de ne ressembler à aucun, évitant avec grand soin surtout que ses réflexions de jeune artiste ne fussent troublées par le contact d'un monde profane, n'en communiquant à personne le résultat, il forma de la sorte ce talent si original, si délicat, si fin, si particulièrement empreint de poésie, pour ainsi dire, aérienne, qu'il a été donné à trop peu de personnes et à de trop rares occasions d'entendre, d'apprécier et d'admirer comme il méritait de l'être. — L'étude seule du piano, quelque développée qu'on la suppose, ne saurait suffire à faire un musicien véritable, dans l'acception la plus étendue de ce mot. — Chopin le comprit de bonne heure; il se fit initier par Elsner, alors directeur du Conservatoire de Varsovie, dans l'art d'écrire, c'est-à-dire qu'il apprit de ce savant professeur les premières règles de ce qu'on nomme la science de l'harmonie. Bientôt l'élève ne parut avoir écouté avec attention les conseils du maître, que pour pouvoir mieux s'en passer, car, dès ses premières compositions, on découvrit en lui un talent d'une singularité remarquable, n'ayant aucune analogie avec les compositions antérieurement connues.

Ce fut en 1831 que, pour la première fois, ce talent se révéla au public. C'était l'époque où la Pologne, essayant par un suprême effort de reconquérir son rang parmi les nations, fut en proie à de si cruels malheurs. Lorsque tant d'hommes dénués de ressources, déshérités de leur patrie, furent contraints de chercher sur un sol étranger des moyens d'existence, Chopin se décida à tirer les siens de l'exercice d'un art dans lequel il excellait, à la vérité, mais qu'il avait aimé jusqu'à ce temps-là de cet amour jaloux dont on aime un objet précieux qu'on croit pouvoir seul posséder à tout jamais. Les premiers concerts publics où il se fit entendre furent à Vienne et à Munich. Il y obtint, comme pianiste et comme compositeur, de si brillants succès, que, vers la fin de la même année, lorsqu'il vint à Paris, il y arriva précédé d'une réputation telle que si la renommée se fût depuis longues années occupée de lui par toute l'Europe. Dès son entrée dans le monde parisien, ces succès furent sanctionnés avec éclat. Le premier concert de sa composition qu'il y fit connaître excita l'admiration générale des artistes et des amateurs ; ceux-ci étaient ravis en écoutant ces phrases mélodiques d'un sentiment exquis, suave, plein de rêveuse poésie ; ceux-là étaient frappés de la forme originale, de la pensée profonde qui distinguaient les divers fragments et l'ensemble de cette œuvre maintenant devenue classique. Les éloges furent unanimes. Malgré cela, Chopin ne put se résoudre à se laisser longtemps applaudir ainsi par la foule. Accueilli avec le plus vif empressement, fêté partout où il allait, désiré partout où il n'allait pas, recherché par ce qu'il y avait de plus élégant et de plus haut placé dans la société parisienne, il se renferma cependant bientôt en lui-même, comme au temps de ses premières années, ou du moins vécut dans un cercle restreint d'amis et d'élèves, qui tous eurent pour lui une sorte d'adoration fanatique, et dans lequel il fut très-difficile d'être admis. Sa constitution extraordinairement délicate était, pour ainsi parler, l'expression visible, très-exacte, de son talent. Le corps le plus frêle qui ait jamais existé servait chez lui d'enveloppe à l'âme la plus immatérielle qu'on puisse concevoir. Cette organisation de sensitive contribuait pour beaucoup, ainsi qu'on le pense bien, à cette espèce d'effroi que semblait lui causer la trop grande lumière de la publicité, à cette horreur de tout bruit, fût-ce même des applaudissements, à cette passion de la solitude, ou tout au plus d'une intimité soigneusement épurée. Et c'était là, dans cette sorte de tête-à-tête, qu'il était le plus admirable à entendre, car il y était tout entier et librement lui-même. Pour la masse du public, il n'a guère été connu que par ses compositions. Le nombre de celles qu'il a éditées s'élève à soixante-dix environ ; les unes sérieuses, les autres légères, toutes marquées au coin d'une individualité extrêmement caractéristique. La plupart, sans doute, lui survivront et feront toujours regretter la perte prématurée de celui qui les écrivit. Frédéric Chopin est mort à Paris, le 17 octobre.

G. B.

Frédéric Chopin, mort à Paris le 17 octobre 1849.

Chopin's obituary from a Paris newspaper, 1849

CANTABILE

Frédéric Chopin

(a) The trill is played on the beat.

N.B. The pedaling is editorial. In the last measure, press the damper pedal *before* playing the last note.

THREE MAZURKAS

**Characteristics
of the
Romantic Era**

Chopin was inextricably linked with his native Poland, as we can hear in his mazurkas. The *mazurka*, the national dance of Poland, is in triple meter, and there is often an emphasis on either the second or third beats. Other musical characteristics of the mazurkas are: the first part of the bar usually has the quicker notes (dotted eighth followed by a sixteenth note), and the scales are often a mixture of major and minor. Chopin also used "Hungarian" scales with augmented seconds. Augmented fourths and major sevenths give mazurkas an exotic character.

Chopin wrote fifty-eight mazurkas throughout his short lifetime of only thirty-nine years. We can imagine that even though Chopin had to leave Poland at the age of twenty-one, he reminisced about his native country for the rest of his life. The romantic term *nationalism* refers to when composers wrote about their native countries and had great patriotism for their homeland, employing musical characteristics of the music of their mother country. This is certainly true for Chopin's mazurkas.

You will find three of Chopin's mazurkas in this volume. The *Mazurka in F major*, Op. 68, No. 3 was composed in 1829 or 1830. In 1830, the U.S. surveyor and engineer James Thompson laid the first plans for the city of Chicago, Illinois.

The *Mazurka in G minor* and the *Mazurka in C major* are both from Opus 67 and were published posthumously (after Chopin's death) in 1855. The G minor mazurka was composed in 1849, the last year of Chopin's life. The first ice skating club in the United States was formed in Philadelphia, Pennsylvania, that same year.

The C major mazurka was composed in 1835. At the same time as Chopin wrote this mazurka, Samuel Morse invented the telegraph, and the first photographs of the moon were taken.

**Characteristics
of the
Romantic Era**

Trills as part of the melodic line:

Trills during the Romantic era do not always begin on the upper note, as is the case during the Baroque and Classical eras. In the Romantic era, trills in a melody that is predominantly *legato* can begin on the principal note, as shown below:

**Practice
Strategy**

Mazurka in C major:

Ornaments in Chopin's music are melodic in nature, and not solely for embellishment or for bravura. If you can sing the trills in the mazurkas in your mind as part of the melodic line, then you will play them correctly. Most ornaments are played on the beat, although exceptions do exist.

"In rapid movement, the trill enlivens or accentuates the note to which it is attached. But in slow movement, more especially in *piano* and *pianissimo*, its gentle dalliance tends rather to soften the blow of the principal note. Here we catch our first glimpse of the important truth that *the effect of an embellishment varies according to the tempo and the character of its context.*"[1]

Practice Strategy

Applying Chopin's *rubato*:

Chopin wrote the Italian music term *rubato* more often in his mazurkas than in any other genre. These dances, which are reminiscent of his homeland, are filled with personal emotion and are a wonderful example of the importance of rubato in the Romantic era. Students of Chopin described the two kinds of rubato Chopin used. In the first kind, the surface rhythm would fluctuate, but never would the underlying pulse. The left hand would "be the conductor," never losing the basic meter. If the left hand is like the trees, then the leaves blowing in the wind is the right hand. If the left hand is a clock, then the player can do what he or she wants in the right hand.

The second kind of rubato is the one that is most familiar, when the tempo fluctuates. The tempo will slow down and then return back to the original tempo. There should be great fluidity in this tempo, and you can count while you play, to hear how the tempo stretches and then goes back to the original. Think of rubato like stretching a rubber band. It always returns to its original shape.

Listen to the mazurkas on the CD and decide what kind of rubato is being used and where. Then you can discuss with your teacher how you would like to approach the interpretation of these pieces.

Let the F major mazurka sound impulsive. Poland was the land of Chopin's dreams, and he had strong, personal emotions about it. Think about what inspires you and what emotions you feel to help you play this piece with aplomb. The G minor and C major mazurkas are delicate miniature poems. The ornaments are part of the melodic line, so play them as beautifully as you can.

[1] John Petrie Dunn, *Ornamentation in the Works of Chopin* (London: Novello and Company, 1921), p. 2.

Mazurka

Frédéric Chopin
Op. 68, No. 3

Allegro ma non troppo (♩ = M.M. 132)

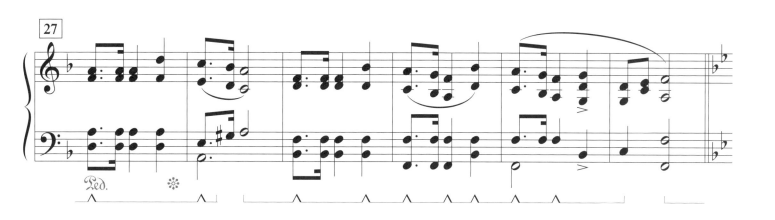

Poco più vivo

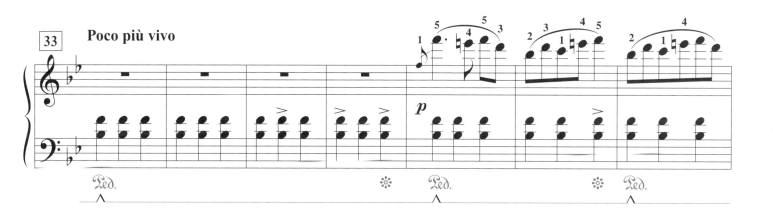

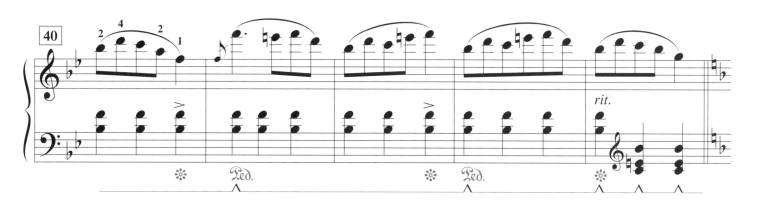

94

N.B. Chopin's pedaling is denoted by 𝒫𝑒𝑑. ✼ and is lighter in color.
The other pedaling is the editor's.

Mazurka

Frédéric Chopin
Op. 67, No. 2

Cantabile (♩ = ca. 108)

N.B. The two longer slurs at the beginning of the piece have been added to show the shape of the phrases.

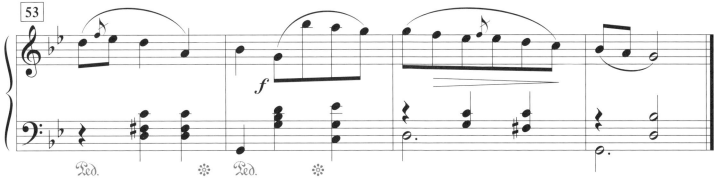

N.B. Chopin's pedaling is denoted by 𝓟𝓮𝓭. ✳ and is lighter in color.
The other pedaling is the editor's.

Pencil drawing of Chopin by Eliza Radziwill, 1826

MAZURKA

Frédéric Chopin
Op. 67, No. 3

N.B. Chopin's pedaling is denoted by ℘ed. ✳ and is lighter in color.
The other pedaling is the editor's.

POLONAISE

Chopin was only seven when he wrote this polonaise. *It is dedicated to the Countess Victoire Skarbek. Her husband owned the land on which the Chopin family had their small home. The Countess heard about the young Chopin's piano playing and invited him to their home to play for distinguished guests. He played beautifully refined pieces, but also played the folksongs of Poland when the Countess asked him to. Chopin's father was a tutor for the Countess's young son.*

Characteristics of the Romantic Era

The *polonaise* was the aristocratic dance of Poland. Polonaises are in triple meter and have short phrases without any upbeat. At the ends of phrases, there is a characteristic rhythm that has an accent on the second beat, as shown below:

Measures 1–6:

Practice Strategy

Practicing "slightly under tempo" or "80% practice":

When you are working toward a performance as a goal, do you ever stumble through a piece instead of playing it flawlessly? If so, the solution is to practice "slightly under tempo," which means to play the piece at a metronome speed 80% of the needed performance tempo. This strategy forces you to be in complete control. It is not a slow tempo, or half tempo. Imagine that every *vivace* is now an *allegro*; every *allegro* is now a *moderato*. You will find as you play at 80% speed that you focus on many things that are spontaneous to you when you play it up to tempo. For example, you will notice the articulations you use with greater awareness, as well as fingering, dynamics, and pedaling. You might be surprised how you listen to yourself play every phrase ending with new awareness and attention to detail. Practicing in this way will give your ear time to listen to every sound you create, and give your mind time to focus on every physical action. If you pay attention to maintain a good, steady pulse during the 80% practice, you will have much more control when it comes time to perform. You can use 80% practice in large-section practice and in performance practice when you play the entire piece. Remember that this is not slow practice, just a little slower to take the edge off and let you feel truly in control. Listen to the practice strategy on the CD in order to understand this strategy even better.

Chopin's Polonaise
By Teofil Kwiatkowski, 1849-1860

Polonaise

Frédéric Chopin
KK IIa/1

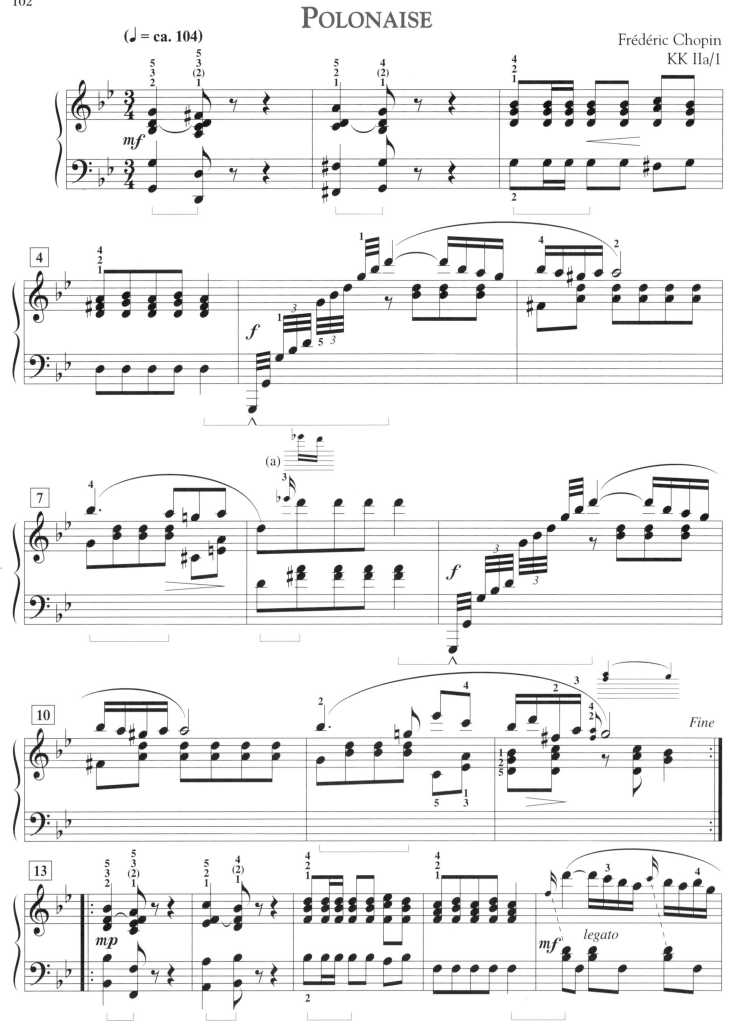

(a) The E♭ is played on the beat.

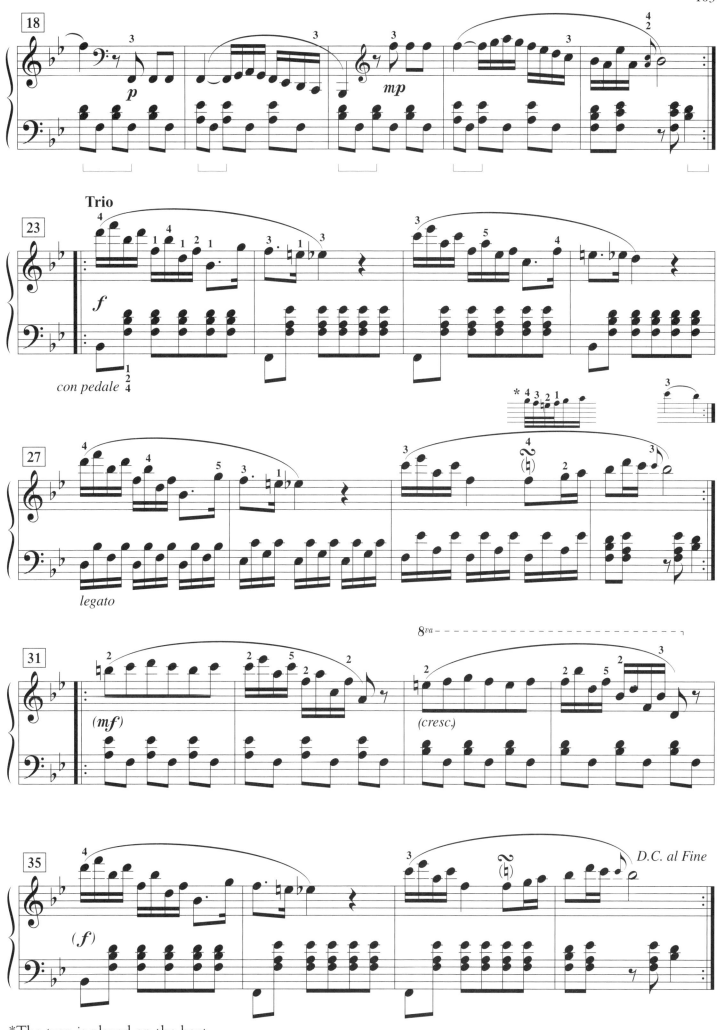

*The turn is played on the beat.
N.B. The pedaling is editorial.

FF1441

LARGO

Largo was composed in 1837, when the world was still lit by kerosene lamps. Cargo railroads were developed seven years earlier and passenger trains four years before. The famous writer of folk tales, Hans Christian Andersen, penned *The Emperor's New Clothes* and *The Little Mermaid.* In America, Martin Van Buren was president, and Samuel Morse invented the telegraph, which is a machine that sends letters in codes made up of dots and dashes. John Deere of Illinois began making horse-drawn plows, and the company he founded became one of the leading makers of farm equipment.

Characteristics of the Romantic Era

Practice Strategy

Drama is an important element of the music.

Using imagery to create a successful performance:

Sometimes it is helpful to imagine a story around the emotions of a piece that you will play in front of an audience. Chopin did not title this work. What emotion does this piece make you feel? You don't even have to tell an audience what you are thinking. Every member of the audience might feel something different, but audiences will always respond to performances that have real emotional content.

In the space provided below, elaborate on one of the following ideas and write your thoughts down.

1. Imagine that this music is part of a movie soundtrack. What scene would this piece accompany?

2. Imagine that you are Chopin, and create a page in your diary describing your thoughts as you wrote this piece.

LARGO

Frédéric Chopin
KK IVb/5

À Madame G. d'Ivry

GRAND VALSE BRILLANTE

By the time Chopin was sixteen years old, he was a famous student at the Warsaw Conservatory in Poland. By the time he left the conservatory, Chopin had written his two concertos and many of his famous études. In 1831, when he was twenty, he moved to Paris. He wrote this waltz the same year. In England, Charles Darwin joined the crew of the *H.M.S. Beagle* as the ship's naturalist. They sailed for two years, mapping the coast of South America.

This waltz has various rhythmic patterns, which were common during the era. Look at the score and notice how Chopin uses triplet eighth notes, groups of seven notes, and triplet sixteenth notes.

A more elaborate embellishment is called a *fioritura*. Notice the following seven-note rhythmic patterns.

Measures 24 and 25:

Characteristics of the Romantic Era

Practice Strategy

In order to play a *fioritura*, make sure that you have an approximately equal number of notes for each beat of the accompaniment. In this group of seven notes, you can distribute the group into 3 + 4. Look at the *fioritura* passage below and notice how it lines up with the bass part. Then look at all of the *fiorituras* in the piece, and with a pencil connect a line from the notes in the left-hand accompaniment to the beginning of each group of notes of the *fioritura*. Your ear will be your best guide as to how to distribute the notes within the triple meter.

When you practice, make sure that your rhythm is precise, and use a metronome often to make sure you have a steady beat. Practice from beats one to two, stopping and listening to make sure that the D♯ in the right hand is played before the second beat of the left hand, and the E in the right hand is played right after. Practice this repeatedly. Then, practice starting on the *second* beat of the measure and going to the next downbeat, listening for the C in the right hand to be played before the third beat of the left hand. Listen to the practice strategy on the CD to completely understand this concept.

À Madame G. d'Ivry

GRAND VALSE BRILLANTE

Frédéric Chopin
Op. 34, No. 2

110

FF1441

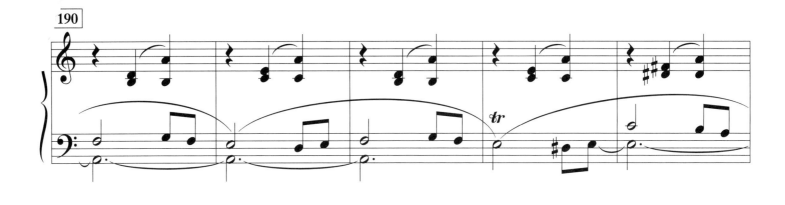

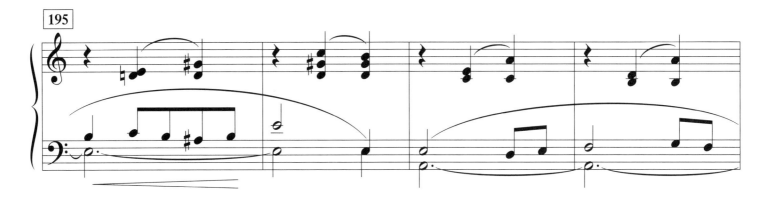

N.B. The pedaling is Chopin's.

VOLUME TWO – REPERTOIRE WITH THEIR SOURCES

FRANZ SCHUBERT (1797–1828)

ROBERT SCHUMANN (1810–1856)

PYOTR (PETER) TCHAIKOVSKY (1840–1893)

The first four selections are from *Children's Album, Op. 39,* also known as *Album for the Young.*

FRÉDÉRIC CHOPIN (1810–1849)

Sources consulted for this edition:

Schubert, Franz. Werke. Kritische durchgesehene Gesammtausgabe. Leipzig: Breitkopf & Härtel, 1884–1897.

Schubert, Franz. Sämtliche Tänze für Klavier, Band 1. Ed. Paul Mies. Munich: G. Henle, 1969.

Schubert, Franz. Sämtliche Tänze für Klavier, Band 2. Ed. Alexander Weinmann. Wien: Vienna: Wiener Urtext, 1973.

Schumann, Robert. Werke, ed. Clara Schumann. Leipzig: Breitkopf & Härtel, 1881–1893. Reprinted by Gregg Press, Farnborough, England, 1967–68.

Schumann, Robert. Album for the Young, ed. Gary Busch. Fort Lauderdale: The FJH Music Company Inc., 2004. (Much of the background information for each piece from Schumann's Album for the Young is taken from this Urtext edition by Dr. Gary Busch.)

Tchaikovsky, Pyotr. Children's Album, Op. 39. ed. Thomas Kohlhase. Fingering and notes on interpretation by Alexandr Satz. Wiener Urtext Edition. Vienna: Musikverlag Ges. m.b. H. & Co., K.G., 2000.

Tchaikovsky, Pyotr. Complete Works, volume IV, ed. Victor Sumarokov and Sergei Chebotaryov. Budapest: Könemann Music, 1998.

Chopin, Frédéric. Préludes, ed. Jean-Jacques Eigeldinger. London: Edition Peters.

Chopin, Frédéric. Piano Works, ed. Ewald Zimmermann. Munich: G. Henle Verlag.

Chopin, Frédéric. The Oxford Original Edition of Frederic Chopin, vol. 1, ed. Edouard Ganche. London: Oxford University Press, 1932.

Chopin, Frédéric. Werke: erste kritisch durchgesehene Gesamtausgabe, eds. Woldemar Bargiel et. al, Leipzig: Breitkopf & Härtel, 1878–1880.

Chopin, Fryderyk. Oeuvres complètes, ed. Ignacey J. Paderewski, in collaboration with Ludwik Bronarski and Jozef Turczynski. Warsaw: Institute Fryderyk Chopin, 1956.

Kornel Michalowski and Jim Samson: "Chopin, Fryderyk Franciszek," Grove Music Online, ed. L. Macy (Accessed 6 February 2006), http://www.grovemusic.com

Elzbieta Witkowska- Zaremba: "Versification, Syntax and Form in Chopin's Mazurkas," Polish Music Journal 3/1 (Summer 2000).

GLOSSARY OF MUSICAL TERMS

Tempo markings

Allegro	*Moderato*	*Andantino*	*Andante*	*Largo*
cheerful, bright	a moderate tempo	a little faster than *andante*	walking tempo	slow, dignified

Accompaniment — a musical background for a principal part. In the Romantic era, the accompaniment can be in another hand, or played with the melody in the same hand. The accompaniment provides harmony for the melody.

allegro assai — a tempo marking that means "even faster than *allegro*." In Italian, *assai* means "a lot of," or "plenty."

a piacere — an Italian term that means "as you like." This means that the tempo, rhythm, and dynamics can be left up to the interpreter of the music.

arpeggio — an Italian word meaning "harp-like." The sounding of notes of a chord successively, rather than all at once.

a tempo — return to the regular tempo, especially after a *ritardando*.

Binary form — a piece built in two parts (AB); the first part sometimes ends on the tonic but usually ends on the dominant (V); the second part ends on the tonic. Both parts are usually repeated.

cantabile — an Italian term meaning "in a singing style."

Chamber music — music played by a small group of musicians (usually three to eight) for small audiences in small rooms (halls). A popular chamber music ensemble during the Romantic era was the piano trio, which is comprised of a pianist, violinist, and cellist. Other important genres are the piano quartet, piano quintet, string quartet, and string trio.

Character piece — a short piano work that expresses a single mood or a programmatic idea.

Countermelody — a musical line different from that of the primary melody. A countermelody can be part of an accompaniment.

Diatonic scale — major and natural minor scales belong to this category. There are five whole steps and two half steps in diatonic scales. In major, the half steps occur between the 3rd and 4th and the 7th and 8th degrees of the scale, without any chromatic alterations. For example, a diatonic A-major scale has the following notes: A B C♯ D E F♯ G♯ A.

Ecossaise — a quick country dance in $\frac{2}{4}$ time.

espressivo — an Italian term that means to play with meaning and emotion.

Exoticism — a musical style in which rhythms, melodies, or instruments evoke the color and atmosphere of far-off lands.

fortepiano — an Italian term (abbreviated *fp*), which means to put merely a slight emphasis on certain notes.

Grace note — a small, ornamental note or set of notes written before a principal note, and played either before or on the beat, depending on the historical period or the musical context.

grazioso — the Italian term for "graceful."

Homophonic — a texture in which a melody is supported by harmonies. The melodic voice is often in the right hand with chords in the left, to create the harmony. It can also be done the other way around, melody in the left hand and chords above.

Ländler — a slow dance from Austria, usually in $\frac{3}{4}$ time.

legatissimo — an Italian term meaning "extremely smooth and connected."

leggero — an Italian term meaning "light and nimble."

maestoso — the Italian term for "majestic."

mano sinistra — the Italian term for "left hand." *Mano destra* means "right hand."

March — a piece with simple and strong rhythm, and regular phrasing. The Italian term *alla marcia* means "in the style of a march."

meno mosso — an Italian term meaning "less motion" or "less quickly."

(N.B.) *Nota Bene* — a Latin phrase meaning "mark well." Used to point out something important.

Nationalism — music which portrays the national identity of a composer.

Nocturne — a piece characteristic of the era that gives the impression of nighttime. Usually there is a melody in the right hand with an arpeggiated bass pattern in the left hand.

Phrase goal — the place toward which the music naturally moves, just as, when we speak, our sentences move toward a word with slightly more emphasis or volume than others. Let your ear be your guide and follow this rise of melody toward a goal. After arrival at its goal, the phrase naturally tapers.

Polyphonic texture — music with several voices (two or more) instead of a single melody and an accompaniment.

Programmatic music — pieces that tell a story or create an image in the mind that corresponds to the title of the piece.

ritardando — the Italian word for "becoming slower," abbreviated *rit.*

ritenuto — the Italian word for "slower, held back." This term indicates a more sudden, extreme slowing down than a *ritardando*.

rubato — the Italian word for "stolen." To stretch or broaden the tempo. However, the time taken is made up within the same phrase or shortly thereafter.

smorzando — an Italian term that means "dying, or fading away."

tenuto — a note that should be emphasized by holding and sustaining longer than the actual note value.

Waltz — a dance in triple time, slow or fast, with one beat in the bar. It first appeared in the late eighteenth century as a development from the German Dance. The waltz was developed primarily by Viennese composers. Precursors to the waltz were the baroque *allemande* and *minuet*.

zart — German for "delicately, tenderly."